SHELDRAKE PRESS
188 Cavendish Road, London SW12 0DA

Published in the United Kingdom by Sheldrake Press Limited in 1991

First edition (Angus & Robertson, UK) 1988
Reprinted 1988
Second edition (Sheldrake Press) 1991
Reprinted 1992, 1993

Art direction and book design: Ivor Claydon and Bob Hook
Designer: Joanna Walker

Illustrations researched and chosen by Karin B. Hills with grateful thanks
to the Colin Mears Collection

Typesetting by Rowland (London) Ltd
Printed and bound in Portugal by Printer Portuguesa, Sintra
Colour reproduction by Fotographics, London/Hong Kong

ISBN 1 873329 04 0

—THE—
KATE GREENAWAY

BIRTHDAY
BOOK

SHELDRAKE PRESS
LONDON

J A N U A R Y

JANUARY

1

2

3

4

JANUARY

5

6

7

8

9

10

11

12

JANUARY

13

14

15

16

JANUARY

17

18

19

20

JANUARY

21

22

23

24

JANUARY

25

26

27

28

29

30

31

FEBRUARY

FEBRUARY

1

2

3

4

5

6

7

8

FEBRUARY

9

10

11

12

FEBRUARY

13

14

15

16

FEBRUARY

17

18

FEBRUARY

19

20

FEBRUARY

21

22

23

24

FEBRUARY

25

_____

_____

_____

26

_____

_____

_____

27

_____

_____

_____

28

_____

_____

_____

29

M A R C H

MARCH

1

2

3

4

MARCH

5

6

7

8

9 _____

10 _____

MARCH

11

12

MARCH

13

14

15

16

MARCH

17

18

19

20

21

22 Linda
66 Axholme Avenue,
Edgware, HA8 5BG
0208 952 2142.

23

24 Beju

MARCH

25

26

27

28

MARCH

29

30

31

A P R I L

APRIL

1

2

3

4

APRIL

5

6

7

8

APRIL

9

10

APRIL

11

12

APRIL

13

_____

14

_____

15

_____

16

APRIL

17

_____

_____

_____

18

_____

_____

_____

19

_____

_____

_____

20

_____

_____

_____

APRIL

21

_____

_____

_____

22

_____

_____

_____

23

_____

_____

_____

24

_____

_____

_____

_____

APRIL

25

26

27

28

APRIL

29

30

M A Y

1 SONIA · 33 Summersby Road
Highgate, LONDON N6 5UH
07957976643

2

3

4

5

6

7

8

MAY

9

10

MAY

11
_____

_____

_____

_____

12
_____

_____

_____

_____

MAY

13

14

15

16

MAY

17

18

19

20

MAY

21

22

23

24

25

26

27

28 Carole Gold · 01707 657185
51 Sunnybank Rd
Potters Bar
Herts EN6 2NN

M A Y

29

30

31

JUNE

JUNE

1

2

3

4

JUNE

5

6

7

8

JUNE

9

10

11

_____

_____

12

_____

_____

JUNE

13

14

15

16

JUNE

17

18

19

20

JUNE

21

22

23

24

JUNE

25

26

27

28

JUNE

29

30

J U L Y

JULY

1

2

3

4

JULY

5

6 Tina Fitzpatrick - 02082006925
83 Frobisher Court
Hazel Close
London NW9 5FZ

7

8

JULY

9

10

11

12

JULY

13

14

15

16

17

18

19

20

21

22

23

24

25

26

27

28

JULY

29

30

31

A U G U S T

AUGUST

1

2

3

4

AUGUST

5

6

7

8

AUGUST

9

10

AUGUST

11

12

AUGUST

13

14

15

16

AUGUST

17

18

19

20

AUGUST

21

22

23

24

25

26 Bridgette Ibrahim
26 Metheuen Road
Edgware MiDDx
HA8 6EX.02089527921

27

28

AUGUST

29

30

31

SEPTEMBER

SEPTEMBER

1

2

3

4

SEPTEMBER

5

6

7

8

SEPTEMBER

9
_____

_____

_____

10
_____

_____

_____

_____

SEPTEMBER

11

SEPTEMBER

12

13

14

15

SEPTEMBER

16

17

18

19

SEPTEMBER

20

21

22

23

SEPTEMBER

24

25

26

27

SEPTEMBER

28

29

30

O C T O B E R

OCTOBER

1

2

3

4

OCTOBER

5

6

7 JOANNA MCFARLANE 67 GRENA RD
RICHMOND TW9 IXS.

8

OCTOBER

9

10

11

12

13

14

15

16

17

OCTOBER

18

19

20

OCTOBER

21

22

23

24

OCTOBER

25

26

27

28

OCTOBER

29

___

30

___

31

___

NOVEMBER

NOVEMBER

1

2

3

4

NOVEMBER

5

6

7

8

NOVEMBER

9

10

11

12

NOVEMBER

13

14

15

16

NOVEMBER

17

18

19

20

NOVEMBER

21

22

23

24

NOVEMBER

25

_____

_____

_____

26

_____

_____

_____

27

_____

_____

_____

28

_____

_____

_____

NOVEMBER

29

30

DECEMBER

DECEMBER

1

2

3

4

DECEMBER

5

6

7

8

DECEMBER

9

10

11

12

DECEMBER

13

14

15

16

DECEMBER

17

_____

_____

_____

18

_____

_____

_____

19

_____

_____

_____

20

_____

_____

_____

DECEMBER

21

22

23

24

25

26

27

28

DECEMBER

29

_____

30

_____

31

_____